Denita,

May God speak to your heart and open your understanding as you read. I pray that this would bring healing & restoration to your life & your seed. Thank you for your support!

P.S. Don't forget to leave an Amazon Review!

Tiffany White

HUSH GIRL!

You Have the Right to Remain Silent in Life's Questionable Seasons

CASSY'S TOUCH PUBLISHING

Scriptures taken from New King James Version and Christian Standard Bible.

Book cover design by SevenFX Creative
Interior Design by Simply Tiffany

Any people depicted in stock imagery are models, and such images are being used for illustrative purposes only.

Published by Cassy's Touch Publishing, LLC
Cassy's Touch books may be ordered through bookseller or by contacting:

www.cassystouch.com

Because of the dynamic nature of the Internet, any web addresses or links contained in this book may have changed since publication and may no longer be valid. The views expressed in this work are solely those of the author and do not necessarily reflect the views of the publisher, and the publisher hereby disclaims any responsibility for them.

ISBN: 978-1-7359222-1-8 (softcover)
ISBN: 978-1-7359222-0-1 (hardcover)
ISBN: 978-1-7359222-2-5 (ebook)

Library of Congress Control Number: 2020919799
Print information available on the last page.

www.simplytiffany.net

Contents

The mouth of the righteous is a fountain of life, but the mouth of the wicked conceals violence.

Proverbs 10:11 CSB

INTRODUCTION

"And He got up and [sternly] rebuked the wind and said to the sea, 'Hush, be still (muzzled)!' And the wind died down [as if it had grown weary] and there was [at once] a great calm [a perfect peacefulness]." (Mark 4:39 AMP)

Muzzled. At first glance, this term can be very offensive to some because it is often related to an animal. However, in this scripture, we see it related to "being still."

In this scripture, Jesus instructed his disciples to get into a boat, and head across the ocean to the other side. After saying this, Jesus proceeded to the bottom of the boat, grabbed a cushion, laid down, and went to sleep. Moments later the weather conditions changed, and the disciples knew that they were not going to make it to the other side. Therefore, in a panic, they woke up Jesus, and the verse above was Jesus' response to the storm.

You will come to seasons in your life where God will instruct you to do something but fails to mention the storm that you will encounter along the way of fulfilling His will. You will find yourself responding to your storm like the disciples did; by fighting for your life, until you realize that *this* storm is out of your league—that is, if you fight from a carnal disposition.

The moment you realize the storm is too strong for you, you turn to Jesus. As He did for His disciples, Jesus will speak to your noisy and boisterous surroundings, and command it to be still—or muzzled.

Then, Jesus turned to His disciples and asked why they were afraid. If they would have operated in faith, then they could have addressed their surroundings themselves.

Jesus was speaking directly to their spirit man and the authority they carried as His disciples. Their surroundings were out of control, but they had the power to muzzle the turbulence.

We are standing in a time where our surroundings seem a little out of whack, but even in this, our identity in Christ has not changed. We have the power to take dominion over every bit of turbulence, yet we still see many who are compromising their authority by speaking according to what they see. When the disciples approached Jesus, they didn't come in faith; instead they only addressed what they saw and felt. Don't forget—Jesus was on the same boat. I am sure He felt the same turbulence His disciples felt, yet He chose to rest.

When the disciples came to Jesus, they spoke according to the effects of the storm. Additionally, they accepted the storm's outcome. They said:

"...'Teacher! Don't you care that we're going to die?'"
(Mark 4:38 CSB)

The disciples accepted the threat that the storm brought. They bowed to the storm and forgot Jesus' initial instruction. The Word of the Lord was to travel to the other side, however when the storm manifested, the disciples accepted death. Their destination was promised to them. It was sure; however, they allowed the storm to alter their vision.

Have you bowed to your storm? If you have, then no condemnation. Simply remind yourself of the Word of the Lord over your life. Reclaim your authority and speak according to the Word of the Lord.

Your words have power. What you speak will manifest. It can either birth God's Word over your life, or delay (even cancel) what is promised to you.

With all that is taking place in our world today, there are times when I had the desire to speak but Holy Spirit would say, "Hush Girl." I am not talking about mindless rambling; I am talking about speaking on subjects and topics that were directly connected to who I am.

So, who am I?

I am young, black, and an unmarried Christian woman living in a culture that is very opinionated. Freedom of speech has never been more prevalent. Thoughts of people all over the world are expressed every second. Household conversations have now become the world's business. Sacredness and confidentiality are scarce and lost within the busyness of the world. Therefore, genuine and authentic friendships are hard to find. Values and morals among people are meager because of what is released out of the mouths of people. Your words create your environment. The environment that we are in today is a result of the words that society has released.

I am young, black, and an unmarried Christian woman who is often misunderstood because not only do I practice celibacy, but I also practice silence. Silence is an art. It is a task. It is a discipline that is only developed through continued self-denial of what you desire to do. Take note: if you do what you desire to do, it will only satisfy you temporarily; however, the consequences are eternal.

It is hard to tame your tongue in a society where there are so many ways to express yourself! You can text, post, shoot a video, post a picture, record a podcast, start a blog/vlog, or even write a book. Even when writing a book, I am restrained from writing what would probably make me feel good because my purpose is always before me. Purpose is always on my mind. People who are wise in what they say have a clear vision of their purpose. They also realize that their purpose is connected to their seed—which is also their legacy.

I don't have to be mindful of what comes out of my mouth—it's a choice. I can be like the majority by yielding to society and the culture of this world; but what would it profit me? How would it support my purpose? Sure, I may gain a few more likes and followers, but what is the purpose of having all of that if I'm just blending in and not making a difference? I am moved by purpose. My mouth releases purpose. When you fully comprehend this, then your language will change.

I am young, black, and an unmarried Christian woman. I am also misunderstood because I'm a millennial. There is a stigma on my generation where research has influenced others to make an assumption on me that doesn't have anything to do with the core of who I am. Sure—I may have the characteristics that are said to be found in millennials because I was born and raised in the same era; however, the core of who I am stems from my Heavenly Father. Statistics can be so far from an individual's purpose. No generation label or stigma can compare to your Godly DNA. The Bible says that we are heirs of God and joint heirs with Jesus Christ. Nothing can change this truth because our identity was solidified when Christ completed His mission on the cross. It is finished.

I am young, black, and an unmarried Christian woman. I am saying this to let you know that although I may not say much, I, too, feel the pressures of life. I am not exempt from it. I am black. I see and *feel* the racial injustices. I have been profiled many times. So of course, my body fueled with anger when that of another race prematurely took the lives of Trayvon Martin, Corey Jones, Ahmaud Arbery, George Floyd, Breonna Taylor, and other countless black lives from this earth. I was angry. My mind flooded with thoughts regarding how my son would be viewed when he comes of age. I thought about my brothers, as well as the other young black men and women I mentor. I was angry, and desired to say a lot. However, I spent more time talking to God than venting to the world. I had to navigate through my feelings and realize that what may be easiest to reach (the world) did not have my answer—God did. Speaking in my feelings would have felt good; however, it had the potential to compromise my purpose. The disciples spoke based on what they saw and felt in that moment. What was the benefit? None. Actually, the storm lasted longer than it should have lasted.

Talking to God heals us, and it prepares us. It always brings change. God is the One Who fuels us to be the change and make the change.

I am young, black, and an unmarried Christian woman. I'm still human, however my identity as a Christian or spirit-being will always supersede what I'm feeling as a human-being. The things that I listed above are all connected to me being human—and there is nothing wrong with all of that because we are living in the flesh. However, your purpose is directly connected to what you allow to manifest through your spirit from the gate of your tongue.

When your perspective shifts from the pressure of this world to the purpose you carry, then you will become more aware of what you allow to leave your lips.

Every season has a purpose, and some seasons are meant for you to… HUSH, Girl!

CHAPTER ONE
AHT, AHT!

I was on a FaceTime call with my mother who was watching my sister's godson (who happens to be a very active and curious toddler). I was explaining a situation on my job when she interrupted me with "Aht, Aht!"

Upon being interrupted with "Aht, Aht," I chuckled. She glanced at her phone, and responded to my chuckle by saying, "He was about to hurt himself." It appeared that this little active toddler was attempting to stand on one of my mother's wooden tables. To stop him in the act, she responded with an authoritative, "Aht, Aht!"

After my mother explained what was happening, I paused, and asked her, "What does 'Aht' even mean? Where did it come from?" She paused, then looked at me and said, "They know what it means!" At that moment, we both began to laugh.

Weeks later, I had a phone conversation with a family member who was in distress. After hanging up with this family member, I began to pray that God would heal their heart and strengthen them. Moments later, I picked up my phone and began typing a text that I thought was very significant to their distress. I was sure that it would help them as they moved forward. As I prepared to press send, Holy Spirit said a resounding, "Aht!" I paused for a second, but I didn't ask any questions; I just cancelled the text message. There wasn't anything wrong with the message I wanted to send to them. Honestly, it may have been of benefit to them; however, as I was shutting the text down, Holy Spirit said to me, "Let Me handle this."

My text may have helped them, but it would have also blocked them from seeing and seeking Holy Spirit. I hadn't done anything wrong, but through my submission to God, I learned that Holy Spirit's voice has a lot more weight than my voice can ever have.

Some things may seem harmless, but if not ordained by Holy Spirit, it can lack purpose and put the person in a worse situation than what they started with. If you continue to be a handicap to them, then they will learn to seek you and not God. Our ultimate goal is to point people back to God.

Think about this: What would happen if they turn to you and you are unable to give them an answer?

God has all of the answers. Sometimes an affirmative "Aht!" from Holy Spirit is necessary for a person to refocus and get on the right track again.

Side note: I cannot believe that I am writing a chapter on the word "Aht," but let's run with it.

When an authoritative power says "Aht", the person who may be in danger, usually stops in their tracks to take a moment to rethink and reconsider their action. As humans, many are guilty of moving on impulse—in other words, without thinking. This is when Holy Spirit comes in to slow you down to rethink and strategize. God's Word says:

"For I know the plans I have for you'—this is the LORD's declaration— 'plans for your well-being, not for disaster, to give you a future and a hope'" (Jeremiah 29:11 CSB)

God's protection will always supersede your knowledge. Sometimes it takes as authoritative "Aht" to stop you from traveling down the road of disaster. This is God's way of protecting you.

However, your response to God's nudging will determine whether you reach destiny or encounter disaster. When you feel a tug from God, it is worth stopping what you are doing to reevaluate your actions, to ensure that you are going down God's path of prosperity and your expected end.

It amazes me that we can spend thousands of dollars on furniture but when it poses danger to someone we love, the cost of the furniture doesn't compare to the cost of our loved one's life or the injury that could occur.

The thought of the wooden table becoming damaged didn't even cross my mother's mind. She was only concerned about this active toddler's well-being. Being that he was in her care at that moment, she was responsible for him. Even if his potential injury was his fault, my mother wasn't going to allow that to happen on her watch. She could foresee what he could not see, or what he chose not to see. My mother saw that this act could harm him. All he saw was opportunity. It took someone else intercepting his act to stop him from injuring himself.

This is how our Daddy God operates. Sure, He made the earth, stars, flowers, grass, and animals of all kind, but your life is what is most important to Him. He sacrificed His Son, to save you. Get this—it does not end at salvation! God will continue to do what He must to protect you, and your destiny in Him.

The Bible says:

"A thief comes only to steal and kill and destroy. I have come so that they may have life and have it in abundance." (John 10:10 CSB, emphasis mine)

This is a well-known scripture. I'm sure that many of you were able to quote it. It plainly states the enemy's purpose for you, and Jesus' purpose for you. Jesus' purpose was to give us life, and God sent Holy Spirit to continue to protect our life in Him.

When you live a surrendered life to God, Holy Spirit will guide you in all things.

I'm reminded of a time where a member of my family showed no sign of sickness, however Holy Spirit urged me to get them to the hospital. Upon arriving to the hospital, the medical staff began to run tests as precaution. Minutes later, the doctor came in and told them, "If you didn't come to the ER today, you wouldn't have been here tomorrow." Holy Spirit is real and guides us in all things. I had no way of knowing what was going on in my family member's body, but God did! His guidance protects your life naturally and spiritually! What a Mighty God we serve!

Galatians 5:25 says that,

"If we live by the Spirit, let us also keep in step with the Spirit."

Being in step with the Spirit is a choice. You must choose to die daily. You must choose to humble yourself under the Mighty Hand of God daily. To stay in step with Holy Spirit, you must choose to ignore the longing of your flesh; or how I like to say it: You must check your flesh! Put your flesh under subjection to the power that lives in you through Holy Spirit. You must choose to be obedient to God. Being obedient to God means that you must learn when to be silent, as well as the significance of your silence.

There are times when the Spirit says, "Aht! Aht!" to protect you from the harm you cannot see. My Pastor likes to say it this way: Holy Spirit gives us insider information. The information He gives you is connected to your life. It is connected with your destiny. You may not have all of the answers but trust His guidance. His guidance brings protection that preserves your life. If you are looking to follow someone whom you can trust, then trust me, Holy Spirit is worth the follow.

The next time you feel obligated to speak out, and Holy Spirit tugs on your "Holy-Ghost-filled" shirt, take a moment to think about your purpose.

What is your purpose?

Is what you say in alignment with God's purpose for you?

Remember that your purpose is not for you—it's for others. How will your words fulfill your purpose and benefit others?

(Write your response below)

_____

_____

_____

_____

_____

_____

_____

HUSH Girl!

_____

_____

_____

_____

_____

_____

_____

_____

_____

_____

_____

_____

_____

_____

_____

_____

_____

_____

_____

_____

_____

_____

_____

_____

_____

_____

HUSH Girl!

CHAPTER TWO

THE QUIET GAME

A husband and wife took a road trip to Washington D.C. to get away from the busyness of life, and to spend some much-needed time away with their two kids. After a failed attempt of going to sleep, the kids began a round of non-stop talking. They named every car, every tree, and even named the colors of the trees. They eventually began asking their parents questions that only the LORD, experienced scientists and environmentalists would know. With his patience growing short, "Dad" gathered up a burst of energy and said, "Let's see who can stay quiet the longest!"

Not knowing any better, the young children exclaimed, "YAY!" The game started and, just like that, peace and quiet.

Can you relate? I think every parent has resorted to The Quiet Game at least one time during his or her time of parenting. The purpose of the game is to give parents a moment of peace to gather their thoughts for the next round of questions that their children will have. On the other hand, the purpose of the game for kids is to challenge them to refrain from talking for a certain period of time—in other words, self-control.

Some kids are quiet for thirty seconds before they become overtaken with the giggles. Other kids may gaze out the window or put their attention on something else and forget that they were even playing the game; however, they are gently reminded that it is still "game on" when they blurt out something that they have seen or discovered.

In the same manner as Christians, God will have us in what I like to call Silent Seasons. In these seasons, there will be things that will prompt a response from you. However, when attempting to respond, you will experience pushback—meaning every time you try to respond to a person or event, something blocks you. Examples would be your call not going through, being interrupted abruptly, the cell phone company's tower being down, your social media post being blocked, you traveling through a wooded area without reception, your car not starting, a family member needing help with something, or your infant having a blowout in their diaper. God will send distractions or will temporarily block you from doing something for the sake of preserving His promise over your life. Something will block you from voicing your opinion; and that something is called God's provision and grace.

Another scenario is that you may feel apprehension when attempting to respond to a person or an event. You may want to give an answer, but you feel an overwhelming unction to remain silent. Can I encourage you to follow that unction? Here is the reason why: The unction that you feel in the pit of your belly is Holy Spirit. Holy Spirit will not lead you astray. In the times where He is urging you to hush, are the times where He is reminding you of the Word over your life. Your response to foolishness (or your response according to your flesh) has the potential of cancelling the manifestation of God's Word in your life. Sister take it from me—in times like these, it is best to hush and pray.

Just like the children in the story above, we are all on a journey. On this journey, there will be seasons where our Heavenly Father will say, "Let's see who can stay quiet the longest!" Like the children in the story, you will get off to a great start but soon after comes your first bump in the road. This bump may catch you completely by surprise. Taken by shock you may say, "Ouch!" then look up to your Daddy. You may wait a few moments for Him to respond when you realize that He is *still* playing the game—total silence.

You are reminded of the game by His silence, and you resume position to remain silent as well. You were doing well until a tall, dark, and handsome man crosses your path. Completely distracted, you begin talking with him—during your quiet season. You both connect through social media and begin talking there. A week or so into your journey with "Mr. Tall and Dark," you realize that he isn't for you. Seeking confirmation on what you feel, you turn to God. God is still silent. You totally forget about the season you are in and become frustrated with God because He isn't answering you. You hope that He responds to your frustration, but He remains silent. Now, you feel as if you are at a crossroad when, in reality, your path never changed; you just became distracted.

Like the game, your silent season is also a time where God develops self-control in you. He will give you instruction at the beginning of the journey, and after that, it is up to you to remember and carry out what He told you.

If you are anything like me, then I'm sure that you are recalling moments in which you thought you were at a fork road, when in reality you were just distracted. You may be here today—where you forgot God's instructions and, ultimately what season you are in; thus, you are on a detour.

Just think:

What if everyone actually waited on God? What if you only moved upon His Word? How would your life look?

This chapter is definitely no condemnation to you, because I'm guilty of running out of God's quiet seasons for my life too. However, this chapter is to bring clarity on where you stand and where you intend to go.

It may seem that God called you to a quiet season at the most uncomfortable moment of your life but trust Him. He has a plan. In fact, He is developing you for His plan. So, what do you do when you are in a quiet season? Watch and pray.

We have many people who are watching and talking, but we don't have enough people who are committed to watching and praying. Instead of telling the world what you see, humble yourself and tell God what you see. The earth is the Lord's and everything in it belongs to Him (Psalm 24:1). He knows what is taking place. He's waiting on those who He is calling to His secret place to respond.

God has so much to share with you. What He shares with you is to prepare you for His next move, and your next season. It is worth you choosing to adhere to God's call and hush for a moment so that you will not miss the promises He has made to you. He is calling you to quiet time to prepare you. Submit to His hand and remain focused, because the season after this one will be worth your decision to hush.

HUSH Girl!

CHAPTER THREE

SILENT MOLD

As a child, I was a huge Play-Doh fanatic! I absolutely loved Play-Doh, Silly Putty, and even slime. Play-Doh took the limits off my imagination. Play-Doh allowed what I imagined become a reality. All I had to do was mold it.

Molding is an act of shaping a liquid or something pliable into a solid object. To mold something means to produce what you have carried in your mind. To mold also means to have control over what you intend to create.

Someone who molds an object has complete control over what they are creating. The object will never live or come to life without going through the process of molding. Molding is a process. Objects that submit to the hand of their creator tend to have the straightest lines, cleanest grooves, and the smoothest bodies. Then the creator can step back, look at his creation and smile. He sees perfection—a masterpiece—all because the object completely submitted to his hands.

There are times where there tends to be a great amount of resistance with our Creator when He wants to mold and shape us. Much of that resistance can reside from your tongue.

Have you ever realized that the things that are easiest to mold don't talk? —Play-Doh, clay, Silly Putty, and dough just to name a few. You have the freedom to mold it however you choose, without resistance.

God chooses to mold you by talking to you. Have you ever witnessed an argument between a parent and their child where the parent was speaking calmly, while the child responded according to their emotions? The parent keeps her composure while the child begins to operate in anger by raising his voice. The parent could have given the child his answer several times; however, the child missed it because he could not hear his parent's response over his emotions.

Many of you reading this are thinking, "Not in my house!" Some of you may have even rolled your eyes while reading it.

I get it—when you believe in honor, it is a natural response to become a little flustered when hearing or reading about someone being disrespectful.

However, Jesus warns us:

"Or how can you say to your brother, 'Let me take the splinter out of your eye,' and look, there's a beam of wood in your own eye?" (Matthew 7:4 CSB)

You may not have been disrespectful to your earthly parents, but how do you respond to your Heavenly Father when you don't get your way? It is probably very similar to the scenario of the mother and son above.

God could be speaking to you; however, you may not be able to hear Him because you are responding according to your emotions. Many miss the details in the molding process because they are unable to hear God's voice over their voice.

You demonstrate submission when you learn how to quiet yourself before the Lord and wait on His leading. It is critical that you exercise this type of self-control in God's molding process because your answer is in His details.

He molds you through your submission and obedience to Holy Spirit. Many do not experience the fullness of God's molding process because their words cancel their submission.

It is very common that God will have you become silent during a time where He desires to mold you. In order to be molded His way, you must be silent enough to hear and receive His instructions. God may allow turmoil to occur in your life for the purpose of you drawing nearer to Him so that He can mold you. He molds you based on purpose. His number one goal is to manifest His purpose through you, and this only happens through complete submission to Him.

Another important factor to take notice of is that clay and putty are soft. The softness creates a better flow within your hand. It moves with your hand.

To be molded we must obtain a soft heart that is pliable to God's hand. Hardness comes from holding onto things that you choose not to let go. Hardness of heart comes from prideful feelings and emotions—not admitting your fault in a situation. Hardness is a place of bondage and not of God.

You must have a desire to move with God's hand.

I have been divorced twice. This is definitely something that I am not proud of, but it is my story; and the shame that easily attaches to divorce has been removed from my story. According to scripture, we overcome by Christ's blood and our testimony. With that said, I declare that my testimony will set you free. I command scales to be removed from your eyes, and your heart be set free as you read this, in Jesus' Name.

It was the Sunday evening after Valentine's Day. My former husband, our kids and I arrived home from visiting my parents. Once the kids were in their room asleep, my former husband walked into the living room where I was sitting. He asked me to come into the bedroom with him because he needed to talk. I could tell from his demeanor that it was something that was weighing him down. Sensing the seriousness of what was on his heart, the walk from our living room to the bedroom seemed like the longest walk ever. Once we entered the bedroom, he sat down slowly on the side of the bed, looked to me and said,

"I think you need to sit down."

I replied, "I'd rather stand."

He looked at me and said, "Okay." He put his head down and took a deep breath. He looked back up at me and said, "Tiff, this isn't working. I want a divorce—"

Before he could finish, I quickly said, "Okay." He looked up and said, "Okay?" I replied, "Yes. Okay."

I stood there like a little girl waiting to be released from the principal's office. He looked me and said, "Okay. I'll begin moving out."

I responded with a very short, "Okay," and left the room. I could not get to the living room quick enough. Why the living room? Because at the time, it was my secret place with God.

I plopped on the sofa, sat Indian style, and looked up at the ceiling. For a moment, all I could do was look up to the ceiling. I heard myself breathing heavily. I finally got enough strength to open my mouth. Tears began to flow down my face as I opened my mouth. I said,

"God.... I don't want to do this again...but if I must... I want to feel every pain in this season...."

I didn't want to be numb. My desire was to feel every pain so that when I came through, I could effectively help someone else because I would be familiar with this type of pain.

This was the moment where I intentionally submitted to God's molding process. This was the season where I learned self-control through my pain. My heart became pliable to God's hands when I told Him that I wanted to feel every pain in that season of my life. Being that I had been through divorce before, I was able to see the effects of going through a tough season without taking the time to feel and digest what I was going through. As a result, I dismissed the healing that could have taken place in my life. I was a little girl in a woman's body who became even more wounded.

The pain felt from my first divorce hardened my heart towards God. I rejected God's healing because I rejected my pain. As a result, my heart was closed off to God's hand.

This time, I wanted change. I refused to repeat the cycle. Asking God to allow me to feel every pain associated with the divorce may be a little extreme for some of you, but I was in a place where I was aware of my purpose and therefore desperate for God's healing.

Now hear me clearly: I am not saying to do what I did, but I *am* saying that at some point of your life, you will have to make a decision to release your will and submit to God's hands. Your life must be pliable in God's hands. I desire the very imprint of God's hands to be seen on my life. What about you? To do this, you must become aware of God's purpose and love for you. Sometimes the pain can be so excruciating that you can barely see God's love; but it is still there.

Because of God's love for you, you can trust that He will defend you. The battle that you are in is not yours; but it *is* for you. The battle is the Lord's, and He is fighting for you. I find that many times people can speak when it is unnecessary, because they feel the need to defend themselves when they are afraid or feel threatened. However, let me reassure you: there is no need to defend yourself. The battle is the Lord's and He is fighting for you.

You may defend yourself by saying that you do not resist the molding process because your resistance is not seen; however, can I ask you a question? What's going on in your mind? If you are in a silent season in your life, your words, or what you would normally say now become your thoughts. Words untamed become thoughts maintained. In other words, your untamed words have now become silent thoughts, which has started a war in your mind.

A mental fight can sometimes be more lethal than a physical fight, because every thought has the potential of setting up a fortress in your mind. If you have fifteen negative thoughts, then you can potentially have fifteen negative fortresses set up in your mind. These fortresses fight against your destiny and ultimately delays the process of God molding your heart.

Can God do anything? Absolutely. However, how you think can stiffen anything that God is trying to do in your life. Jesus was in the height of His ministry and Bible says that Jesus didn't do many miracles because of the people's unbelief (Matthew 13:58).

In addition to submitting to God physically, you must also submit to God mentally in order to maximize your silent season in Him. It's not enough to just silence your tongue, but you must also silence your mind from breeding negativity. You must train your mind to think on things that are conducive to your purpose.

Do me a favor: Take a deep breath. Exhale. Take another deep breath. Close your eyes. Exhale. Receive God's peace and whisper, "I'm safe." Take another deep breath, and release. Rest. Rest your mind, and rest in His Hands.

You will find safety even in seasons where you are being molded. Just take a moment to hush girl. You are safe.

HUSH Girl!

CHAPTER FOUR

HUSH AS A LEADER

I've had the pleasure of being under a few people who have selflessly invested in my life to see a better "me" arise. This type of investment required my complete trust in their words, and submission to their guidance.

Here is a little fact about me: Growing up I was known to be a little stubborn. However, as I grew older those stubborn ways left, and developed into tenacity and a strong will. I didn't give up easily. If the verdict said that it couldn't be done, then I would do all that I could to demonstrate that it could, in fact, be done. Since then, I have balanced into a more intentional, mature, and productive individual. I do not give my attention to things where it is not required. I intentionally protect my energy because I have learned that when you are focused on fulfilling your destiny, you will need all of the energy you have to accomplish it.

Prior to this awakening, I lived in a way where I felt I had to prove people wrong. I felt it was my duty to remain loyal to the statement "anything is possible" when all others gave up hope. However, this lifestyle took up large amounts of my time, energy, and mental capacity. At times, it drained my natural ability to create. I was low on creative juices often because my energy was invested in a place that was not conducive to my destiny. I had to be delivered from this lifestyle and mindset because although it was harmless to others, it was very harmful to my destiny.

I overcame and gave my stubbornness to the LORD, but I never lost that inner determination and passion; and, to this day, I am very strong-willed (with wisdom) and my energy is connected to things that revolve around God's purpose and destiny for my life.

Now let's rewind a bit. Picture this: a stubborn girl who would not move when her mind was made up; accompanied with a dash of feistiness, and a dose of sassiness. I was that girl. (God did a thing when He made this girl).

To say the least, submission nor trust came easy for me. To submit meant to give up my control, and to trust meant to give up defense mechanisms—all of which became a strategy of how I navigated through relationships. God knew that I needed help in these areas so that I could reach my destiny, and it would require me accepting the help sent by Him. Sounds easy, right? I thought so, but receiving help required me breaking my old lifestyle by submitting to and trusting those whom God placed in my life.

When God created me, it was through His infinite wisdom that He also created a package plan that would help me reach my destiny. In that package plan were people who were assigned to groom me professionally, spiritually, mentally, and physically.

Can you identify those people whom God placed in your "package plan?"

I'm grateful for the people in my package plan because considering my old ways, it would appear that I wasn't built to be mentored or invested in. Why? Because in order to follow effectively, you must know how to submit and trust who you follow; and this little lady didn't trust many people with her whole heart.

Additionally, I was stubborn and my out of control sassiness made my responses to constructive criticism lethal. I operated on the impulse of my emotions, and my mind ran with those emotions. It took me days, sometimes weeks, to grasp the meaning of the constructive criticism given. My emotions tore me down before I allowed the love of trusted individuals to build me up.

What is now clear was once hidden by pride. I couldn't identify the places I needed healing, because I operated from the place of the victim. You will have instances where some people truly are victims, but you have some that have developed a victim mentality because they failed to heal from the first offense. This victim mentality breeds entitlement, which is another form of pride. It's hard to be mentored when you're prideful. A word of caution for you: Choose to heal and humble yourself—because eventually something will break you where you will have no other choice but to be humble.

My mentor also happens to be my spiritual mother. Her print on my life is huge. I'm convinced that many people would have given up on me during my healing process because of how toxic I was, but she put on her mask and chose to love me to wholeness—even in the trenches. Now being aware of how much of a "project" I was, I'm indebted to her for her unwavering labor of love.

Through my process, I often found myself in tough situations where I sought the LORD and shortly after I sought my mentor. I would often feel that I needed an answer from her because she would always know what to do. However, she soon realized how much I was leaning on her. She saw that I was leaning on her so much; that I did not trust what she knew was imparted in me. I didn't trust what I was taught. I was equipped, but I did not trust the equipment. I wasn't confident with using the new tools that were inside of me. In my eyes, she was experienced with the equipment, so I knew that she had the wisdom and answer I needed.

I was insecure with my tools.

Think about a toolbox. My Dad had a few toolboxes. As kids, my siblings and I would quickly purchase the go-to gift for Dads. Whether for Christmas, Father's Day, or his birthday we resorted to what we thought, Dad's would love—new tools. It was the answer to all Dad holidays! My Dad would gladly accept the new tools given, however when things needed repair, he would retrieve his "trusted" tools. There was this favorite hammer or screwdriver that he would always seek out when he felt like the "new tools" weren't accomplishing the job. The new tools had the same purpose, but he had a greater trust and confidence in the older tools. Those tools were proven. He knew how to use them, and he would rather use what he knew how to use than to learn how to use something new.

Something similar happens with us. We fail to acknowledge the purpose on the inside of us because we lean on what or whom we know. When you rediscover you, it's like having a new set of tools. In other words, there is a side of you that is untouched; and instead moving in the new and untouched side of you, you'd rather pull on those in your life who are proven. Walking in "newness" is a learning process.

We see many people excited about receiving "the new"; but once you receive it, you must be committed to the learning process. What good is receiving something new if you never use it? That, which is not used, loses its purpose.

My mentor saw this happening in me. I began to realize that when I presented different issues to her, she would become silent. Not rude. Just silent. Her choosing to be silent was another place of development for me. I had to look at what I knew, acknowledge what I didn't know, and become acquainted with the newfound tools within me. It was uncharted territory. At times, it was very uncomfortable because I felt like I was making the biggest mistake or decision of my life. It was a risk, but healthy development requires that we take risks. It was necessary. In order to access what you have; you must be challenged to look for it. Don't let your gift, wisdom, and calling go undiscovered because you never took the time and risk to look within.

My mentor saw my weakness of leaning on her in times of uncertainty and committed to watching me develop trust in what God placed in me.

There were times when I called her, laid out my problem, and she listened. After I finished unloading, I waited for her response but all I received was silence. One day after going through this routine, I boldly said, "I don't know what to do." She responded, "And I'm not telling you because you do."

I tried to convince her that I really didn't, but she stood strong in her stance. I submitted, and guess what? She was right. I was uncomfortable in making the decision, but I found that I had gathered enough substance over the years to address the situation wisely.

Those words remained with me, and eventually shifted me from riding with training wheels to trusting that I have the capability to remain balanced while moving.

My mentor led me even in her silence. Her silence caused me to search within only to find untouched tools that were ready to be used.

I liken this to a father guiding his child as they learn to ride a bike without training wheels.

A little girl loved riding her bike. She was confident riding her bike as long as the training wheels were on. She depended on the training wheels to stabilize her; however, there came a time where her father saw that she had enough practice with the training wheels and was capable of balancing by herself. One day, he chose to remove the training wheels from the bike when his daughter was not looking. Once he finished, he went into his daughter's bedroom and asked, "Do you want to ride your bike?" She answered with excitement, "YES!"

She hurried to put on her shoes and walked outside with her father. Once outside, she looked over to where her bike was parked only to find that her bike no longer had training wheels. Her excitement left her immediately. She looked up to her father and said, "I don't want to ride anymore."

Knowing that she was only speaking from a place of fear, her father gently replied, "Baby, you can do this." The father's eye was never on the bike; his eye was always on what his daughter was capable of doing.

She trusted her father's word. The little girl grabbed the handles and rested her bottom on the bike seat. She looked back at her father and asked, "Are you going to hold it?"

He smiled and nodded, "Yes." She attempted to pedal but could not get her footing due to her losing her balance. Frustrated, she abruptly got off the bike, and let it fall to the ground. Her father walked over and said, "What's wrong baby?" The child crossed her arms and said, "Hmph! I can't do it!" The father rubbed her back, and then whispered, "Let's try one more time."

Trusting her father's word again, the child walked over to her bike as her father picked it up. She got on. He held the back of the seat as she placed her feet on the pedals and began running with her as she pedaled. Feeling a little more confident, she took her focus off her feet, and looked ahead to where she was going. When the father saw her focus shift, he silently let go of the seat, and stopped running. He stood back proud as he watched his daughter do what he knew she could do all along.

My mentor made the tough decision to take my training wheels off and let go. I was apprehensive because my life was very unstable up until that point. I was not confident that I could maintain the balance that I acquired without her giving me the answers. Her silence allowed me to see my inner strength, and my ability to navigate through life as a balanced individual.

As a leader, you will have seasons where you must be silent. Choosing to give the answers to your followers all of the time will stunt their growth. Every good leader has the goal and purpose to see their followers grow and become leaders themselves. In order for this to manifest, you must be okay with being silent for a season.

As leaders, we see and know the potential of our followers to a certain extent; but there is much more that remains to be seen. There is a power that is hidden. There are things that your followers possess that are not revealed until you choose to HUSH.

HUSH Girl!

CHAPTER FIVE

DON'T BE ANXIOUS

It's easy to become excited and anxious about the things that God is doing in your life. Beware: Don't allow that excitement or anxiety to lead you to speak out of God's timing.

I am reminded of when Jesus began His ministry here on earth. He moved in miraculous ways where thousands of people were healed even at the sound of His voice. You can imagine how excited these individuals became where what they struggled with or carried for years was gone in a moment. They were ready to tell someone about what Jesus did for them; however, Jesus urged them not to tell anyone.

Why? Why would Jesus restrain them from sharing the best thing that has ever happened to them with others? Whenever you have something good happening, or if you are in a period of waiting, it is easy to become anxious. It is easy to share every little detail with those you love. You are bursting from the seams with anticipation, waiting to release details of what is taking place in your life to the whole world. However, if it is revealed before its timing, then it could backfire.

Jesus knew that the Father operated in timing. He was pressed many times to reveal who He was, but He stood in God's timing. He even told His mother that His "...hour has not yet come." (John 2:4). If His very own mother could not get Him to move out of timing, then you know how important it was to Him to prioritize God's timing.

Some things must wait before you choose to advertise it. Premature advertising can lead to a compromised purpose.

I recall a time when a relationship of mine reconciled. I was so excited that I decided to share my testimony with the world (aka Facebook). Upon sharing, a friend texted me privately and said:

"I'm so happy to see that you all are together... however don't be so quick to share this with everyone quite yet."

Now most people would have probably asked her, "Why? Do you know something that I don't know?" Not me. Overwhelmed with joy and filled with religion, I replied with a real "churchy" answer, not acknowledging the sign that she gave me. My reply went something like this:

"Thank you! We are so excited, and God is so great. We are confident that God will finish the work that HE started."

I spoke according to God's Word and everything sounded good; however, it did not change the fact that my "reveal" was out of God's timing.

The Apostle Peter admonishes us to,

"Be sober-minded, be alert. Your adversary the devil is prowling around like a roaring lion, looking for *anyone* he can devour. (I Peter 5:8 CSB, *emphasis* mine)

Although the enemy is not as harmful as a roaring lion, the Apostle Peter says that he has tendencies as a roaring lion.

Why did the Apostle Peter compare the adversary to a lion? Let's take a deeper look at this. When lions hunt, they do not hunt alone. Therefore, the first thing that you need to take into consideration is that when the enemy lurks, he is not alone. When lions hunt, they have a proven strategy; everyone is given a role. One lion looks at the prey (we will call her the leader), and the other lions are watching her. Once the leader locks in on the prey, the other lions take notice of what has caught their leader's attention and shift their focus in the same direction. They do not make a sound; they only use their eyes to communicate.

Here is the second take away. Just because you revealed your business, does not mean that the enemy will reveal himself immediately. His attacks can catch you by surprise because he and his entourage strategize silently. They do not make a sound or cause commotion before their attack. This is why it is so important to keep your spirit aligned with Holy Spirit because He will give insight that will prepare you before the attack.

This is how lions lurk. They lurk with strategy before revealing themselves as the predator. The enemy is the same way—he lurks with strategy. He watches first to see what weaknesses you reveal, and then he casually makes his move, followed by a sudden attack by his entourage.

The good news is that we have already overcome, but we must always be alert because he is lurking somewhere.

I learned the hard way. I bypassed the knowledge of a friend and innocently covered it by saying, "I trust God." However, I did not consider that the people watching and "casually" liking my posts, could have had ill intentions, and spoke against what I revealed. I revealed it before the true identity of who we were was solidified in our hearts. Therefore, we were not able to overcome the backlash that came our way in many forms. Needless to say, that relationship soon dissolved.

It is important that you do not become too ambitious or anxious that you reveal your identity before it is accepted in your heart, because there will always be backlash. You must be at a resolve to use your strength (mentally, spiritually, and physically) to resist the enemy. The Apostle Peter continued by saying:

"Resist him, firm in faith, knowing that the same kind of sufferings are being experienced by your fellow believers throughout the world." (I Peter 5:9 CSB)

To resist the enemy, you must have a knowing. You must know who you are, who he is, his tactics and strategies, and most importantly, Who God is. Our victory rests in God's Name and Character. If you do not know Who God is, then be intentional in learning about Him so that you are able to stand "firm in faith" as the Apostle Peter instructs us to do.

Do not be so anxious to share what God is doing in your life with others that you slip out of God's timing. Instead, take it to God first. He will let you know when it is time to reveal.

God is a God of order and time. I'm sure that He could have created an embryo so that its parents could know its gender at conception, but God saw that the time for development was necessary before the reveal. Not everything has to be revealed immediately. Embrace your period of development before you share with the world what God is doing in you.

The Apostle Paul tells us:

"Don't worry about anything, but in everything, through prayer and petition with thanksgiving, present your requests to God." (Philippians 4:6 CSB)

Take it to God and He will give you the green light on if or when you can share with the multitudes. People who are waiting in expectation of things often ask, "Well, how will I know when I am released to share?" Good question and I wish that I could gather words to give you the correct answer. However, the truth of the matter is that you were created with instinct.

When a mother nears the time of delivery of her child, she unknowingly enters a stage called "nesting."

I experienced this firsthand. My son was not due for another three weeks however, I had a sudden urge to complete all of my household tasks, which included sweeping my courtyard, washing all the clothes and linens, cleaning the kitchen and bathrooms, and the list went on. I had entered the nesting phase of my pregnancy. I felt like I had to get those things done, and I had to do it quickly. The amazing thing in all of this was that God did not give me the desire without giving me the tools. With my sudden urge to prepare, I also obtained an extra dose of energy to complete the tasks. It is supernatural. Little did I know that a few days later, I would be welcoming my baby boy into this world! I had no idea that my son would make his arrival so soon, but my instinct prepared me for what I didn't know.

You will know when it is time for you to release. God will begin preparing you for the arrival of your "news," and not long after that, you will know that the time has come.

Do not be anxious. HUSH and prepare.

HUSH Girl!

CHAPTER SIX

SILENCE REVEALS

Pornography. Sex. Perversion. These were things I felt I did not have an issue with. This, of course, was until I found myself sitting still, caught up in an online teaching series. This series uncovered a root in my life that I did not know existed.

Some people consider it normal for kids to go through "the changes"—which includes the interest of the opposite or same sex at a young age. However, what is seen in children can be the residue of unresolved issues in the bloodline. If "bloodline issues" are not confronted and resolved, then what you see in your children *may be viewed as normal* being that you experienced it and turned out "fine." However, just because you experienced it and came out "alright," does not make the struggle normal for your legacy.

As a young girl, I struggled with embracing my femininity and developed an attraction to females. The attraction did not last long nonetheless, it existed. Once I began embracing my feminine side and became attracted males, I was out of control. I felt that I broke through what was considered wrong (desiring the same sex), and as a result I fully embraced my attraction to men—the more men the better. I thought that I was delivered from my past when in all actuality, I had just left one phase of my struggle and entered the next. I never took the time to deal with the spirit behind my behavior. Truth is, the pleasure in my lifestyle was not found in whether I was attracted to males or females, but it was found in the feeling that I received from it.

Although I was not attracted to the same sex anymore, I was involved in multiple, sexually active relationships with the opposite sex at once. The "church girl" in me would not allow me to have sex before I was married, but there was a lot of foreplay in between.

Bottom-line: I struggled with the spirit of perversion. However, I was blind to my struggle because my bloodline counted it as "normal." It was not until I got under a ministry that taught on this topic, that I was able to identify my struggle. Can I be honest? Even when I became aware of my struggle, I fought to deny it. I did not want to become another person in church who struggled with the hidden sin (which really isn't hidden) of perversion. I was no longer sexually active, but I still was found "talking" to several men over a short period. Becoming more aware of my struggle daily, I quickly adopted a busy lifestyle as a way for me to remain hidden. However, that did not last for long.

One day my mentor called me and stated that she wanted to take me to lunch. Excited at the thought of being able to spend time with her, I happily accepted. However, I learned very quickly that this was not going to be a "chill" moment.

Once we ordered our food, she looked at me and said, "Tiffany, what's going on?" (I learned that whenever she asked this question, the LORD showed her something that I have not accepted or that I was still oblivious to). I just looked back at her in silence; I was lost as to what she was relating to.

She continued, "Why are you giving yourself to all of these men? You may not be physically 'sleeping' with them, but you have given them access to who you are, and they're not even connected to your destiny."

Our server returned with our food and, needless to say, I suddenly loss my appetite and needed a to-go box. This conversation shined the light on my dysfunction that I disguised as normalcy. "Talking" to several men at once or in a short period was not normal. It was actually the residue left on my life from the spirit of perversion. In that moment, my struggle literally slapped me in the face. I could no longer deny it.

I had to find some quiet time to take a deep look at myself and locate the root of my struggle. In my quiet time, I came across an online teaching series that shined the light on the root of my issue. In that moment, I accepted the place where I stood in my struggle and committed to break the cycle. This cycle stopped with me.

If you want to be free, then you have to be bold enough to ask yourself the following questions: What is your normalcy based upon? Is it aligned with God's normalcy, or is it in harmony with the standards of this world? Like me, you may avoid answering these questions because it risks you opening up a painful season of your life; however, if you desire true freedom and wholeness, then you must take a risk on yourself and ask.

Half of the things that are considered normal in life are so far from the truth of God's Word, and His heart. Your normalcy could be your place of bondage.

Sometimes people stay bound because they are too busy to remember what they have chosen to forget. I have found that, many times what you have chosen to forget is actually the root or key to your deliverance. However, roots can only be revealed through complete participation in God's process, which is normally found in your silence.

When you become silent, you become obedient. Your silence leads you to a contract with God that simply says "YES,"—because now you are able to accurately see and hear what He wants to reveal to you.

God's desire for you is to live an abundant life here on earth, which is why He sent His only Son, Jesus, to die for you. He never intended for you to live a life of bondage. He has promised you freedom. Your freedom begins with you getting quiet and listening for His voice.

As you listen, may your heart give God a gentle, yet affirmative yes.

Yes Father, I acknowledge my sin. Yes Father, I am not perfect. Yes Father, I see the root. Yes Father, Deliver ME! Yes Father, I am ready to be free!

Freedom is yours! Receive it! Your yes will lead you to deliverance, which leads to freedom. And this is all made possible because you chose to HUSH.

HUSH Girl!

CHAPTER SEVEN

PURIFIED SILENCE

"...Casting all your cares on Him, because he cares about you." (I Peter 5:7 CSB)

Living in today's fast-paced world, you can unintentionally take on its cares and worries. This type of lifestyle is not a part of God's original intent for humanity. God created us so that we would naturally need Him. He created us so that He could work through us, however we do not see the works of God as often as we should because many who are called by God, are weighed down with today's cares.

There was a challenge that was circulating on Social Media not too long ago, that was called the #ThenAndNow challenge. Those who participated in the challenge would find a picture from ten years ago and compare it with a recent picture to see how much they have changed. I rarely participate in challenges, but I participated in this one. When I began to look at pictures from ten years ago, I began to reminisce about that time. Every picture had a meaning attached to it. I was able to captivate the feelings that were felt during that time.

As I continued to reminisce, I took note of how things have changed. Photos were for memories, and not solely for likes. The only foods available for delivery were Chinese food and pizza. These are just a few things I remember about life ten years ago without getting too personal.

Although at a slower pace than today, the speed of life was still increasing back then. We live in a fast-paced world that is full of distractions. People spend hours on the computer, and if they come across time to be still, they do not know how to quiet their mind. The world has gradually taught us to think about what is next; but there are times where God will postpone or delay what is next so that He can purify you now.

The pressure that comes from living in this fast-paced world makes it very easy to move on impulse. It can seem as if you are in constant competition with the world. Social media has given you the opportunity to see the lives of many up close and personal, where sometimes you can unknowingly take on the challenge to do better than the next person—my mother used to call it "keeping up with the Joneses." If you are not careful, then you can easily enter a competition that was not assigned to you. A sense of "I can do that too," or "I can do better than that" is developed when no one asked you in the first place!

No one sent an invitation for you to participate in this competition; however, you invited yourself to the races because you still struggle with the spirit of performance.

As I write this book, we are in the midst of a world pandemic. The coronavirus has become an unseen enemy that has claimed the lives of thousands. The way in which it spreads from one person to another has been its driving force. It is easily transmitted from one person to the next, and as a result, we have had to adjust our lives drastically with social distancing measures, including the mandatory use of facial masks.

In the spiritual realm, the spirit of performance is very similar to COVID-19. This spiritual virus has infected generations and cultures for years. Left untreated, this spiritual virus will continue to be passed down from generation to generation.

So, how do you address the spirit of performance? As it is with all other spirits, the spirit of performance rises from a root issue. To identify root issues, you must make a conscious decision to get quiet before the LORD. Additionally, you must choose to be intentional about embracing what God reveals to you.

I find that when we are presented with the ugly parts of who we are, we tend to walk away in denial—telling ourselves that we heard wrong. Ninety-nine percent of the time you have heard right, but your flesh would rather not accept the ugly.

Whenever you get into God's presence, remember His character. As stated in an earlier chapter, God's plan and intention is for you to prosper, and give you hope. God never presents anything to harm you; instead, He presents the ugly to purify you.

Now, this does not mean that the process of God revealing these things to you won't hurt—the truth always hurts. However, your pain does not come from God, but, rather, it comes from how your flesh responds to God's truth. Truth kills our flesh, which can be painful. The Bible says:

"For the flesh desires what is against the Spirit, and the Spirit desires what is against the flesh; these are opposed to each other, so that you don't do what you want." (Galatians 5:17 CSB)

The Apostle Paul writes:

"Therefore brothers and sisters, in view of the mercies of God, I urge you to present your bodies as a living sacrifice, holy and pleasing to God; this is your true worship." (Romans 12:1 CSB)

Holy Spirit residing on the inside of you is your direct connection to God. As stated in Galatians, the Spirit is at war against the flesh; therefore, in order to align yourself with God, you must choose to present yourself as a living sacrifice to God. This means that you must deny your flesh and submit to Holy Spirit daily. Submission means to accept what God trusts you with, to accept what He reveals to you, and allow Holy Spirit to do the work.

God only reveals to heal. What He reveals normally starts in silence. If you are seeking purification and sanctification, then I admonish you to learn the art of humility. Submit to God's hand. This can be done when you choose to HUSH Girl.

Was there something in the chapter that caught your attention? Did something ignite your spirit or bring clarity while reading? Use the space below to write down three takeaways from this chapter. How do you intend to apply it to your life?

_____

_____

_____

_____

_____

_____

_____

_____

_____

_____

_____

_____

_____

_____

HUSH Girl!

_____
_____
_____
_____
_____
_____
_____
_____
_____
_____
_____
_____
_____
_____
_____
_____
_____
_____
_____
_____
_____
_____
_____
_____
_____
_____
_____
_____
_____

HUSH Girl!

CHAPTER EIGHT

SILENCE REQUIRES NO EXPLANATION

As stated in my introduction, I am an unmarried woman. I have been single for a little over three years now. However, in my time of singleness, I have "talked" to a couple of men. There was a time where the LORD called me to silence in the midst of me trying to get to know a young man. I communicated with him that the Lord was leading me to a time of silence. His response was, "Great! How can I pray for you?" I stated that I was unsure. He responded, "Okay. So, does this mean communication needs to be at a minimum?" My response was, "Yes." He understood without explanation.

Of course, others did not understand and wanted an explanation regarding my silence. I did not explain my sudden move for several reasons, but perhaps the greatest reason was that *God* had not given me a reason—He had only given me instruction. You will experience times in your life when God gives you instruction without reason, and your relationships must be solid enough to trust you as you commit to trust God.

There will be times where all you will feel is a heaviness or weight in your spirit, accompanied with a pulling away from what is normal. These instances can happen suddenly, and it is something you cannot afford to ignore. You cannot wait until you receive clarity from God, because many times your clarity is found in your "pulling away" or quiet time.

I believe the times where God does not give you a reason for "pulling away," is to show you that *He is* the reason. He desires your full attention. When you do not have the answers, then you must seek God. I believe that the best posture for learning is knowing that you don't have all the answers. Operating in this posture will increase your curiosity, and hunger for wanting to know more.

We can also liken this to on-the-job training. Your experience must be in real-time (in other words, up close and personal) to prepare you for what is next. This "training" will prepare you for the next time when He sits on you with or without explanation. Yes—there is a possibility that God will call you to silence *and* give you a clear answer as to why He is calling you; however, He may still instruct you to not share His reasoning with others. Some things must remain sacred until it has become developed enough for the world's response. If endured well, then the "training" without explanation, will prepare you for those future times when God gives you an explanation *and* instruction not to share.

You must be okay with not giving people a reason for your obedience to God. Your obedience to God does not require an explanation, but *it does* need your full and complete participation. God can call you to a sudden time of seeking for many reasons. It can be a time where He calls you to prayer, or a time where He desires to renew your focus.

Ninety-nine percent of the time when God calls you to silence, it is so that He can speak to you. He desires your undivided attention. It is in these times where you cannot allow your mind to become cluttered with thoughts of how people are viewing you in response to your sudden withdrawal from them. When God calls you to solitude, you cannot compromise your time by giving attention to things that do not matter. You will navigate a little easier when you are able to come to a resolve that nothing (and I mean absolutely nothing) matters more than the presence of God.

It is during this time that God shows you the benefits of your uninterrupted time with Him. It is worth a temporary misunderstanding. People who are not intimately acquainted with God will misunderstand "God moves," and possibly make it all about them. Do not fall into that trap. Your silent moments are ALL ABOUT GOD—period. Do not expect everybody to understand at that moment but do expect everyone to respect you and the authority you will carry when you come out of your secret place with God.

Your obedience to God is their example to follow. We are all leaders in some capacity, and God has assigned a group of disciples to each of us. Look at Jesus' life. He had many followers; however, He only had twelve disciples. There were times where He had to withdraw from the twelve disciples He was leading, to get into the presence of His Heavenly Father. This was necessary for Him because it was significant to Him leading others effectively. To lead effectively, God's presence is necessary.

Do not compromise your leadership for a moment of acceptance from others. Leaders make tough decisions for the betterment of others. You must understand your leadership and all it encompasses. Jesus had a clear understanding of what God required of Him as a leader. He knew the purpose of why God assigned those twelve disciples to Him. Do you have a clear understanding of your leadership? Do you know why God assigned your "disciples" to you?

Let me help you: Your disciples' assignment to you is connected to your purpose. Once you are clear on your purpose, then everything else will fall into place.

Do not fall into the trap of explaining why you do what you do. True disciples and those connected to God understand that your pulling away is necessary not only for your development, but also for their development. Time spent with the Father does not go wasted.

Understand that you do not need to explain your silence. Your obedience will always be greater than what you sacrifice. You will always come out with new understanding, ideas, and answers. You will always leave God's presence with something new. The sacrifice of silence is worth it. HUSH.

Do *you* have a clear understanding of your leadership? Do you know why God assigned your "disciples" to you? Take a moment and write down your purpose in the space provided. How does your purpose relate to you leading others? My prayer is that you become clear about why God has you here, and intentional in your service to others.

_____

_____

_____

_____

_____

_____

_____

_____

_____

_____

_____

HUSH Girl!

HUSH Girl!

CHAPTER NINE

SILENCE
DOUBT

One year I faced a very complicated situation. The LORD was requiring much that I was not sure that I could give. This involved me speaking up and making moves on behalf of my safety which, in turn, ruffled the feathers of others. In that moment, I was challenged to do what no one else would do. I was challenged to be the difference.

Being the difference is simple when you have people standing with you, but standing alone is a completely different feeling. I believe that the people who were involved in my situation knew that the treatment I received was wrong; however, since no one confronted them for their wrong in the past, they were never challenged to change.

It only takes one to disrupt a narrative causing others to take another look; but that one must be courageous enough to stand when no one else is standing. God chose me to be the one.

There were many days where I would run to my car to retreat in between dealings because I was literally in a battle. I was at odds with a few colleagues who were not letting up in their stance, and God would not allow me to let up in my stance neither.

This was a big deal for me, because I was never a person to confront anyone about anything. I stayed away from confrontation, even if it was to my detriment. I would silence my needs to accommodate the demands of others. This type of behavior was developed because I had a tainted perception of what peace was.

My understanding of peace was keeping people happy by avoiding necessary conversations. If you are living this way, then I pray that God removes the scales from your eyes because this type of living robs you of your peace and healing. Some conversations must be had to bring healing, as well as clarity which results in peace.

We see a number of individuals who struggle with illnesses because they have tried to keep the peace by avoiding situations and conversations. Let me help open your eyes to what is really happening.

When you avoid having necessary conversations, you will end up internalizing what you need to release. This reminds me of the significant functions of our kidneys and bladder.

The kidneys and bladder work hand in hand. Once liquids enter our body, it is filtered through our kidneys, which removes waste, and produces urine. The bladder drains the urine from the kidneys and stores it until it is released. If the kidneys stop functioning, then the bladder will no longer have anything to draw urine from, and your body risks the chance of toxins entering it.

If you avoid necessary conversations, then what you have internalized will continue to intoxicate your thinking, behavior, actions, and perception until you decide to filter through what you need to release. You will become drained and will not have anything to draw from.

When done with maturity, confrontation brings peace. Confrontation is the thing that stirs the unknown or ignored and brings it to the forefront. We need confrontation for the sake of peace.

God delivered me from my old way of thinking and since then, I have experienced freedom in a new way.

Although uncomfortable, I knew that my stance was right because Holy Spirit led me there. The doubt only set in when I began to turn my attention to self. I would often times find myself in silence when I retreated to my car. As I sat to reflect on the situation, I began to ask myself if I was overreacting, or if I was right by standing strong in what I believed to be right.

I was strong when it came time for me to stand, but when alone, I began to have silent doubts. Whenever you begin to have silent doubts, you must be careful that they do not evolve into mind battles. When you doubt, you are feeding the nature of your humanity; because truth is, you are incapable of winning spiritual battles without Holy Spirit. Doubts flooded my mind because I did not have a place to physically release it at that time. Little did I know God's divine strategy behind His plan was to eliminate other sources where I would normally release, so that I could to turn my attention to Him. My victory and strength to endure was found in Him. I had to understand that the battle that I was in was not initiated by me; therefore, I could not draw on my own strength. The Initiator of the battle was Holy Spirit. I was only the vessel He used—therefore, I had to draw from Him.

You need God to win this battle. You cannot afford to walk in doubt by turning your focus on you. Your focus must remain on God. We are powerless without God. When in battle, people may not care about what you have to say, but they must bow to what God says.

If you are in a spiritual battle, then do not let doubt stop or delay you from making progress. Silence your doubts and turn your focus back on God. I pray for a second wind to come upon you now, and that all doubting and self-sufficiency would leave you now in the Mighty Name of Jesus. I pray for Godly wisdom to fall afresh upon you now. I command all anxiety, worry, and tension to leave your presence now. May the presence of

God surround you. He is your Source and your Safety in the time of battle. He is Jehovah Shalom, your peace. May you receive an inner peace now, in Jesus' Name. Amen.

Walk in your authority as a child of God by telling your doubts to HUSH!

HUSH Girl!

CHAPTER TEN
SILENT FEARS

I have a place in my home where I love to sit while working. It's a brown microfiber sofa located in my living room. This sofa is made to seat three people comfortably; however, my laptop, electronics, Bible and other study materials normally take up the extra space. In this spot, I am able to look out of my sliding glass window and watch neighboring families walk by. I also enjoy watching the slight breeze make the branches of the trees sway back and forth. Sometimes I am able to see the slightest movement, such as a beautiful reddish-orange pedal of a flower float onto the pavement in response to the wind.

One day I sat in this spot, gathered my laptop, study Bible and prayer journal. I was ready to begin working (so I thought). As I sat in this place, I could not move past the silence. I glanced out my window, and I began to ask God, "Why am I here? Why am I unable to move forward with my agenda?" I felt as if I should have been doing something else—perhaps studying as I had intended to do—but He stopped me in my tracks. I continued by asking, "Why Father?"

As I began to ask why, He responded by flashing my future in front of me. I saw success and was immediately overcome by fear. Fear had gripped my heart at the thought of me messing up what He revealed. Then, fear began to tell me that I would not be able to accomplish what I had seen. I began to feel my body shrink, falling back into the mold of the "not being seen and unnoticed" mentality and posture.

Let me put a pin there. There is a difference between being silent and being unnoticed. Many times, becoming silent is in response to something, while being unnoticed is an internal battle that springs up from the fountain of pity. Falling into this posture shows a detachment of purpose. It is also a sign that you really do not have clarity of who you are, and the power that you have.

I hear some of you saying that you are clear on who you are, but it seems that people still are not noticing you or your purpose. This, my friend, has everything to do with God's timing. This is not being unnoticed; this is being overlooked. David was a powerful servant and warrior, yet he was overlooked for years. However, being overlooked did not take from nor minimize his purpose. He stood in the fullness of who he was until God revealed him to the right people. I speak more about David's life, and being overlooked in my book, *The Court, The Camp, The Throne*.

Once I became aware of how my body and mentality was responding to what God revealed, I quickly regathered myself and began to speak according to God's purpose for me. Fear is a spirit that will silently keep your destiny trapped for years. Although fear silently traps, its effects and impact on a person can be loud and blatant. Once you become aware of fear in your life, then it is imperative that you identify the root and eradicate it immediately.

Fear has paralyzed nations, leaders, families and even Pastors. There can be a tangible presence of success and favor on a person however if their heart is gripped with fear, then they will only see a fraction of what God has promised them.

We can no longer be passive about the Spirit of Fear. It has claimed too many lives. Your life, destiny, and legacy are counting on you to silence your fears and move in the promises of God.

Even now, I declare that you will move in the favor of God. You will be successful. Your seed will be successful. You will boldly walk in the promises and purpose of God. No demon or devil will be able to stop you, because the presence of God is with you. I declare Jehovah Shammah is with you and shall be your rear guard. No evil shall come near your dwelling. You shall experience overflow. I decree that you will walk in the fullness of your healing, and I decree that your body will be made whole; your mind will be whole; your spirit will be whole in the Name of Jesus.

Go get what belongs to you. God keeps His Word and never fails. Stand on that and remember what God promised you. I declare that you will be successful once you tell your fears to HUSH!

HUSH Girl!

CHAPTER ELEVEN

SILENT WAIT

"Be still, and know that I am God; I will be exalted among the nations, I will be exalted in the earth!" (Psalm 46:10 CSB)

This scripture is one of my life mantras. Like many of you, God has taken me through seasons where I had to wait. Some seasons I had to learn the hard way by attempting to do things on my own until I submitted to God's gentle Word: "Be still and know that I am God."

I knew that He was God all along, however my unction to move without Him was because I felt that I had waited long enough. I had reasoned with myself by thinking that there was no way that God would want me to wait *that* long for something He promised me. However, I failed to acknowledge the purpose of my wait. You see, the wait was never about me—my wait was all about God's purpose being revealed through me.

The scripture above tells us why God desires for us to wait. We wait so that He can be exalted on platforms that exceed our reach. His wait is for our development. God is not concerned as to whether His promise will come to past; He is concerned if you will be able to carry the weight of the promise.

The period of your waiting season depends on how submissive you are to God's hand. The truth be told, God can manifest His promise without your cooperation, however His desire is for men to know Him before Christ's return, and this is done by them having an example to follow. You are the example.

Your season of waiting is necessary because it serves as a place of preparation and development to be that example.

"Humble yourselves, therefore, under the Mighty Hand of God, so that He may exalt you at the proper time, casting all your cares on Him, because He cares about you." (I Peter 5:6-7 CSB)

It pays to humble yourself and submit to God the first time He tells you to do so. People who struggle with pride often lack development because their behavior is "too loud" to hear God tell them to sit down so that He can do the work that is required before exaltation or promotion. It can take prideful people three or four times of getting it wrong before they capture the reason behind their period of waiting.

Many times, I would find myself moving instead of waiting on God, and when things did not pan out the way in which God previously shared with me, I would return to God and ask Him why. He would not say anything; instead, He would remind me of what He originally told me to do: Be still and know that I am God.

When you maintain a spirit of humility, you may not fully comprehend the reason behind God's instructions, but you must be obedient to Him regardless. If I may speak from experience, God does not change His instructions for the season just because you decided to take a different route that makes sense to you. The Bible says:

"There is a way that seems right to a person, but its end is the way to death." (Proverbs 16:25 CSB)

The Bible also says:

"A person's heart plans his way, but the LORD determines his steps." (Proverbs 16:9 CSB)

You may have plans, but at the end of the day, it is God's plan that stands. If your pride keeps you from submitting to God's way, then He will wait until you have exhausted all of your options and you have to turn to Him. This is why it is important to ensure that all your faculties (mind, spirit and emotions) are in line with God. You will find that when you are aligned with God, then your plans are God's plans.

When you ignore God's instructions to wait, then you extend your time of waiting. Obey God the first time.

When God becomes silent in your time of waiting, then go back to the last thing He spoke to you and meditate on that. I have found that whenever God speaks, it is to reveal something about us. If you are too busy to digest the Word spoken to you, then you will miss the purpose of the Word.

Periods of silent waiting is for your development. I can understand your eagerness to exit out of your waiting seasons; but can I encourage you to "Be Still?" Life may be very noisy but be still. Your vision board is screaming at you but find time to be still. God remains silent, because He desires that His presence speaks to you in the still moments. The answer that you are seeking is found in His presence.

In Psalm 16, we are introduced to David declaring that God is his Refuge. He also acknowledges God's sovereign protection. David reveals his complete dependence on God by declaring that although he is the king, the only good thing that he has is God. David makes it clear that God is his Source. He expresses that although he may encounter trouble and torment, his focus will remain on the LORD. Then he says:

"You reveal the path of life to me; in your presence is abundant joy; at your right hand are eternal pleasures." (Psalm 16:11 CSB)

Not only does God reveal the path of life, and give you joy in His presence, but His presence also gives you pleasures that reach past what this world can give! He does not have to speak; His presence says all and solves all.

Your answer is not necessarily in His voice; it is in His presence. Answer God's beckoning the first time by being still in His presence. Do not look for answers; seek His presence. You will find everything that you need in His Presence.

When you are waiting in silence, shift your focus from what you desire to what God desires. Ask God to give you a hunger for His will being accomplished in your life and wait for Him to reveal His path to you.

Your path is simpler than you think—all it takes is you humbling yourself, seeking God's face, and embracing His presence. Your silent season of waiting is the pathway to God revealing Himself to you. The key is to get into His presence by telling your plans to HUSH.

Let's jumpstart your time with the LORD. In the space below, journal your thoughts and plans. May this be a way for you empty yourself so that you can receive everything that the LORD has for you as you seek Him.

HUSH Girl!

HUSH Girl!

HUSH Girl!

CHAPTER TWELVE

SILENT DEPRESSION

I didn't want to get out of bed. I had zero motivation to do anything because I didn't have the answers to the turmoil that was taking place in my life. All I heard was silence. My mind tormented me, and it was a struggle to do what Philippians 4:8 tells us to do:

"Finally brothers and sisters, whatever is true, whatever is honorable, whatever is just, whatever is pure, whatever is lovely, whatever is commendable—if there is any moral excellence and there is anything praiseworthy—dwell on these things." (Philippians 4:8 CSB)

I knew this, however dwelling on those things were not in my immediate reach. My current situation gripped my mind, and controlled my thoughts so much, that my mind could not grasp the simplicity of what the Apostle Paul was instructing Philippi to do. I was in a hard place, which triggered a war in my mind.

In prior years, the battle always took place in my mind, but I overcame that way life. Yet, I found that there will be some situations in life that may put you in a place that is contrary to who you are, and in order to get out, you must do what is required naturally so that you can regain your strength spiritually.

In first Kings Chapter 19, we find Elijah in a dark place. The Bible tells us that Jezebel set out to have Elijah killed because God moved in a miraculous way through him, turning many hearts to the LORD. In response to Jezebel's threat, Elijah ran into the wilderness, sat under a tree and prayed,

"...I have had enough! LORD, take my life, for I am no better than my ancestors." (I Kings 19:4 CSB)

Elijah was fed up with life. However, in that moment God sent an angel to tend to Elijah's natural needs. The angel touched Elijah and told him to get up and eat. Elijah ate and went back to sleep. The angel returned a second time and told Elijah to:

"...Get up and eat, or the journey will be too much for you." (I Kings 19:7 CSB)

Elijah had given up, but God sent an angel to keep him alive. Elijah did not want to continue, but God provided so that he could get out of his slumber to continue. Elijah's assignment would not let him die. God had to tend to Elijah's natural need so that he could live *and* complete the journey before him.

I was in a dark place like the Prophet Elijah. It was a place that had the potential of paralyzing me from pursuing my future. It was a hidden place. I struggled with the shame of letting others know that I was back in the place I once overcame. I needed help like Elijah.

As servants of God, it is important that you are not so caught up in the assignment of serving people that you forget to serve yourself. Self-care is necessary. I echo the words from the angel of the LORD, "Get up and eat (or care for yourself), or the journey will be too much for you." The life we live and the weight that comes with it is real. You are not a superhero, so do not try to be one. Instead, grab a hold to God's grace.

The Apostle Paul also found himself in a hard place. He was tired of the thorn that was lodged in his flesh. He was tired of feeling the agitation and pain that was associated with this thorn. Therefore, he pleaded three times for God to remove it. God's response to Paul was:

"...My grace is sufficient for you, for my power is perfected in weakness..." (II Corinthians 12:9 CSB)

The answer to resurrecting a dead mentality is to accept God's grace for you. His grace releases power and stamina in your life to accomplish what you cannot do on your own.

Forgetting that I was *not* a superhero, I fell into depression. Within this depression was a hint of frustration, irritability, and anger because I was tired. I was tired of getting ahead only to come to an abrupt stop.

However, I never voiced my anger, which is how this anger and frustration evolved into depression. Internalized anger is depression.

My mind was fighting to retain the Word of God. I desired to move on His Word regardless of what I was sitting in. It is in these times that the only strength you have is strength to make a choice to move forward. It will take all of the strength you have to do what Elijah did—to decide to get up and keep moving.

This was the answer I needed to overcome my funk. All I needed to do was to make a choice. If you are in between a rock and a hard place, then I want to encourage you that the key to moving forward is making a choice to do so. Can I share a secret with you?

You are not stuck; you just do not have an answer yet. Not having an answer does not mean that you are stuck and cannot move forward. However, you do need to trust. Trust is making a decision to move forward even if you do not have all of the answers.

Many times, people become stagnant in tough situations because they are deceived of their true power. The enemy comes in to tell you that you cannot move forward because you do not have clarity. Let me expose this lie and remind you that:

You can do ALL things through Him who strengthens you. (Philippians 4:13 CSB, EMPHASIS mine)

In summary, people become paralyzed when there is a disconnect between their mind and their body. The enemy attacks your mind because he knows that if he can convince you that you are stuck in your mind, then the rest of your body will follow.

I encourage you to break your state of paralysis and choose to stand on God's Word. Rely on His strength to move forward. Use the little strength that you have to move forward. One of the most powerful things we can do is make a choice; and I guarantee you that God gives you enough strength every time to make the right choice.

Silent Depression revolves around a choice. Move from your paralyzed state by choosing to tell the enemy to HUSH!

HUSH Girl!

CHAPTER THIRTEEN

SILENT BIRTHING

According to Google, the definition of birthing is the action or process of giving birth, or the action of an emergence of new life. Webster's Dictionary defines it as an emergence of the new from a parent body.

When a woman goes into labor, she has the responsibility to remain committed to the process as her body prepares to birth what she has carried for nine months. Believe it or not, her body has a responsibility as well. A woman's body must remain consistent in the birthing process. The body must make steady progress as the new life emerges.

When I was pregnant with my son, I was looking forward to experiencing labor and all that came with it. Clearly, I was new to the game. My obstetrician told me early on that natural birth probably would not be an option for me because of my body frame, and the size of my baby. Nonetheless, I still believed that I would have my baby natural and informed my doctor the same. Although apprehensive, my doctor respected my wishes.

Three and a half weeks prior to my due date, my son had an expected weight of nine pounds and seven ounces. My doctor was concerned because he was running out of room to move, and we still had almost a month left until my due date. Another concern was that I was contracting, but my body was not responding to it. Therefore, the doctor convinced my former husband and I that it was best to have a cesarean section to ensure that the baby and I remain healthy.

My body had a responsibility to respond to the birthing process by preparing the way for my baby to enter this world. My responsibility would have been to remain committed as my body went through the process. Whether you are aware of it or not, our bodies respond to the atmosphere around us and within us. Sometimes the body develops ailments and illnesses in response to what is going on in a person's life. When I was going through my divorce with my son's father, I was on seven different medications. Three of the medications were for anxiety and depression. The ailments experienced was the manifestation of how my body was responding to the divorce. I felt as if I could not control my body's reactions, therefore the medications were prescribed to regulate my body's reactions.

There are people who have never experienced depression or anxiety; however, with the weight of the current pandemic as well as the effects of racism, I know several people who are now on medication for anxiety. Although silent, the body responds loud and clear when placed under pressure or stress. The body cannot physically talk without the life of a soul, but it can respond.

When you are in a time of birthing, you must remain committed to the process. You must also ensure that you are in an environment that is conducive to responding to what you are about to birth.

Silent birthing may be a time of pain and discomfort because God is clearing the way to make room for what He is about to release through you. Making room means that God may have to remove relationships that you thought would last forever, or He may lead you to make huge sacrifices. All is intended so that you and your vision can flourish at the time of delivery. Your pain may become so intense that it may take your voice away during the birthing process, but if you remain committed to the process, then you will eventually see that the pain was worth it. You will see what God was preparing you and your environment for all along.

It is so important that you are obedient in your time of birthing. This may mean that God may abruptly deliver you from a situation that is detrimental to what you are carrying. You must remain obedient by silencing your curiosity of why God allowed disruptions to happen to you. You cannot afford to chase what God has strategically removed. Everything that God does is attached to your future, therefore you will not have understanding of God's ways all of the time.

Your focus can determine the intensity of your pain. The night before the birth of my son, I was laying in the hospital bed when the nurse came in to check on me. She and I were talking when all of a sudden, she glances down at the paper that was tracking my contractions. She slowly looks up to me, and says, "You don't feel that?" I look back at her confused and say, "Feel what?" She responded, "You just had a pretty good contraction." I said, "Oh. No, not at all." She made a few other comments and left the room. Just because I did not feel the contraction does not mean that it was not there. However, my expectation was no longer on a natural birth. I was anticipating a cesarean section. Therefore, my focus was no longer on the process and pain that came with giving birth naturally.

At times, your pain may seem worse than what it is for the simple fact that your focus is on what you are experiencing now. However, God does not work in the now—He is always a few steps ahead of us. He goes before us. The Bible says,

"For My thoughts are not your thoughts, nor are your ways My ways,' says the LORD. 'For as the heavens are higher than the earth, so are My ways higher than your ways, And my thoughts than your thoughts." (Isaiah 55:8-9 NKJV)

You are literally walking out what was already planned and established for your life. I encourage you to do as the writer of Hebrews instructs us to do:

"Therefore, since we also are surrounded by so great a cloud of witnesses, let us lay aside every weight, and the sin which so easily ensnares us, and let us run with endurance the race that is set before us, looking unto Jesus, the Author and Finisher of our faith, who for the joy that was set before Him endured the cross, despising the shame, and has sat down at the right hand of the throne of God." (Hebrews 12:1-2 NKJV)

Can I encourage you? You may be in an uncomfortable spot. You may be experiencing pain but set your attention of Jesus. He was able to endure the cross and the shame because His eyes never left God. His focus did not take away the pain that came with the process, but it strengthened Him to endure the pain. When your eyes are on God, then nothing will stop your progress. Your life, destiny and future are in good hands. You are safe in Him.

Hard changes precede the emergence of new life. God is silently changing your surroundings and environment, so that what you carry will thrive once delivered. God has equipped you to move in greater works. The pain experienced on the road to greater may be intense, but it is my prayer that you will not lose your focus during this time. In fact, I command every distraction and spirit that was meant to thwart your destiny to HUSH now in the Name of Jesus! Amen.

HUSH Girl!

CHAPTER FOURTEEN

SILENT FAITH

There was a season in my life where I faced a tough decision that had the potential of affecting my well-being, as well as my son's. I believed God for a miracle. I wholeheartedly believed that He would work on my behalf where things would turn in my favor. Meanwhile, I was doing all I knew to do until God performed.

One day, I ran out of options and I faced making a decision without having much clarity. I was solely depending on God to work my situation out however, when it did not work out as expected; it fell back in my lap. Overwhelmed with stress, I went to my car and sat in silence. In that moment, my heart was too overwhelmed with the cares of my situation for me to try to formulate words to say to God. I did not know what to say. I was at a loss for words and sitting with no direction.

In my silence, the LORD whispered this in my ear:

"What will you sacrifice for My purpose without question?"

Notice that He did not ask what I would give up for His purpose; He asked what I would sacrifice for His purpose. There's a difference. I can buy someone a gift according to their interests, and trust that they will love it. If it does not appeal to my interest, then I can give it to the person without any struggle. I can easily give what I do not want to someone else without thinking twice about it. However, a sacrifice is attached to who you are. What is considered a sacrifice definitely has your interest; however, that is just the surface level of what a sacrifice is. A true sacrifice is giving up something that is embedded in who you are.

Sacrifices are tough. Sacrifices are of special value to you because you have labored over it. You have history with it. You have a genuine love for it. Sacrifices are detachments of things you treasure for the benefit of someone else.

Abraham faced a tough decision. He waited several years until He had the son that God promised him. Shortly after Abraham received his promise from God, God instructed him to terminate the promise. Abraham was obedient and took the journey to sacrifice Isaac (his promise), however I believe that Abraham had a close enough relationship with God to know that he could not ultimately terminate what God promised him. He could not terminate God's promise because God honors His Word and promises. Abraham may not have been clear as to how God was going to honor His Word, but he knew that God would honor His Word.

I can imagine that as he approached the place to sacrifice his son, the more expectant he became of how God was going to come through for him. He did not say much, but each step was a demonstration of his faith in God. Sometimes the pain from your sacrifice will have you at a loss for words, however, do not let that stop your progress in God. Keep walking, because your faith will increase to another level with each new step.

When the time came for Abraham to sacrifice Isaac, he heard the voice of the LORD tell him to stop and directed Abraham's attention to the ram that was caught in a bush. Abraham was able to hear God, because he was silent in his journey to the mountain.

When in a tough situation, it is important that you eliminate all distractions and interferences—even if that interference is your own mouth. You must do what it takes to keep your spiritual channel clear so that you can accurately hear God when He speaks.

The children of Israel complained while in the wilderness. As a result, their journey lasted forty years. What if they chose to be silent in their journey? Would they have reached the Promised Land?

Sometimes you have to remain silent when placed in uncomfortable situations and allow your feet to demonstrate your faith. It is important that you do not lose sight of God's Word over your life when you face tough, life-changing decisions. His Word will give you the strength to walk out your journey, even when it hurts.

God asked me, "What will you sacrifice for My purpose without question?"

While sitting in agony, this question realigned my thinking. Yes, I was in an uncomfortable position. Yes, where I stood was very painful, but it was all attached to His Word and purpose for my life.

When faced with a difficult decision, choose to remain silent, but never stop walking. Keep your feet moving, because at the end of it all, what you sacrifice is for His purpose. God has to honor the Word that He speaks over you. The only way you will see His Word manifested in your life is if you choose to keep moving in faith when everything else is telling you to stop.

God is going to provide. God is going to release His answers, but it will take silent faith to get you there. HUSH!

HUSH Girl!

CHAPTER FIFTEEN
SILENT SURRENDER

I typically listen to prayer music in the morning as I work. One morning as I was listening to my music, I began to think about the tough situation that I was facing. It seemed as if I kept hitting a wall when I attempted to move forward. I began feeling bound and restricted by my situation, which made progressing more difficult.

I am what the world calls "a creative;" which means that I am at my best when I have an open canvas. With that said, moving while restricted can be extremely difficult for me. I am all for boundaries given the situation, however I have difficulty comprehending why a boundary is in place when there is not a reason given to justify the boundary.

I was in a season of life where there were restrictions without reason. Daily I fought hard to obtain clarity, but no one could give it to me. Looking back on the situation, I don't know if the individuals who were involved knew why they were adamantly pushing against me. While in this season, I often asked God why?

I would receive Words from the LORD that were in my favor, which would build my hope; however, the actual outcome seemed to be opposite of the Words that my spirit received. Therefore, I was not questioning God's authority, but I asked for the sake of obtaining clarity as to why the Words spoken over me were not manifesting. I wanted to know what I was doing wrong. Why didn't I see what was prophesied over me?

This was a spiritual battle and with every battle, a strength is revealed. The LORD saw the battle, and He saw that His daughter was undeveloped in some areas. Sometimes God will allow battles to exceed "your timeframe" to develop you. The best part is that He does all of this while keeping you safe. He sees you, He sees your fight, and He sees your end. As long as you stay in the hands of God, that place that is undeveloped in your life will be revealed and strengthened.

There is a posture that you must have to win life's battles. You can't change your battle posture until you shift your battle perspective.

"For we do not wrestle against flesh and blood, but against principalities, against powers, against rulers of the darkness of this age, against spiritual hosts of wickedness in the heavenly places." (Ephesians 6:12 NKJV)

You must shift your perspective from thinking that the attacks you are experiencing are carnal, to acknowledging that every attack has a spiritual source.

"For though we walk in the flesh, we do not war according to the flesh. For the weapons of our warfare are not carnal but mighty in God for pulling down strongholds, casting down arguments and every high thing that exalts itself against the knowledge of God, bringing every thought into captivity to the obedience of Christ," (II Corinthians 10:3-5 NKJV)

When your perspective changes, then your purpose will arise. You will acknowledge the source of your battle, and the Source of your weapons. Your weapons are not carnal, but instead they are created for you to wage war in high places. Your weapons are only mighty in God.

I had to come to a place where I silenced my carnal weapons. My carnal weapon was my tongue. I confided in my friends and family; however, my battle was so intense that I didn't talk to them for a period because I would run the risk of them unintentionally igniting my carnal weapon. When your perspective changes, then your posture will shift. You will make adjustments that will shout "By all means necessary, I will see the goodness of the LORD in the land of the living." I had to come to a place of desperation to see God's promise for me manifest in my life. So, I made the adjustments necessary that would minimize compromise. I silenced myself.

This posture brought about humility to bow to God's hand. The Apostle Peter said:

"Likewise you younger people, submit yourselves to your elders. Yes, all of you be submissive to one another, and be clothed with humility, for 'God resists the proud, but gives grace to the humble.' Therefore humble yourselves under the mighty hand of God, that He may exalt you in due time, casting all your care upon Him, for He cares for you." (I Peter 5:5-7 NKJV)

God gives grace to the humble. The grace you need to get through this battle is accessed through humility. He will exalt you in due time. So, there is no need to panic or worry. Instead, give God all that you carry and rest in His hands. Your victory is in your ability to rest in Him.

I found rest in God. This rest is what I like to call my "sweet spot." I used to play basketball, and every shooter has what I call a "sweet spot." It is in this spot you know that you will make every shot without effort. You don't worry about missing it because it is your guaranteed spot. It promises a point. In the same manner, when you learn how to rest in God, you create your sweet spot in Him. This place in God is a place where you are free of worry and anxiety because you know that your victory is guaranteed. When you are presented with difficult situations, run to the Rock. Find your "sweet spot" and rest in God. Your "sweet spot" in God promises a guaranteed win. He never loses.

As I sat at my desk in my frustration, the hymn "I Surrender All" began to play. As I began to sing the words, I felt the boundaries that were very present in my situation breaking. As they broke, I broke. I fell into His arms and accepted His rest. At that moment, I felt the coolness of God's presence comfort me. He whispered, "Silent Surrender." We can have inner peace even in a war; however, this peace is only found when you acknowledge the Source and surrender to Him.

I've found that many people resist surrendering to God because it means that you no longer obtain control of your situation. God gave us all free will so *you can* choose to take control; but take it from someone who has done it their way for years: taking control will not benefit you at all. One reason it won't benefit you is because you don't know what your end looks like in its entirety. Only God sees the full picture, and He is the only One Who can get you there safely. This battle is worth your surrender. To help you get there, I took the time to write out the lyrics to the hymn *I Surrender All*. May you experience the freedom of resting in God's arms as you give voice to these words.

"I Surrender All"
Author: Judson W. Van De Venter (1896)

All to Jesus I surrender
All to Him I freely give
I will ever love and trust Him
In His presence daily live

I surrender all
I surrender all
All to Thee, my Blessed Savior
I surrender all

All to Jesus I surrender
Humbly at His feet I bow
Worldly pleasures all forsaken
Take me Jesus, take me now

I surrender all
I surrender all
All to Thee, my Blessed Savior
I surrender all

All to Jesus I surrender
Make me Savior wholly thine
May Thy Holy Spirit fill me
May I know Thy power divine

I surrender all
I surrender all
All to Thee, my Blessed Savior
I surrender all

HUSH Girl!

CHAPTER SIXTEEN

SILENT SERVING

Perhaps one of the most painful seasons of my life was when I had to intentionally serve in pain (mentally, emotionally, and spiritually) while being silent. Daily I had to fight off the demons of depression and push past my pain to serve others with excellence.

I didn't realize it then but every time I served as unto the LORD, I was activating my faith—and my faith was opening doors without my knowing.

One morning, my mind was saturated with the situation at hand. In that moment of hopelessness, Holy Spirit spoke to me, "Silent Serving." He made it clear that my service *and* the quality of service was not dependent on what I was feeling in my flesh. There was still a requirement and standard that God was holding me to.

The upkeep of my body and my overall health is important to me, so I work out daily. One day while working out, I began to reflect on my situation and I said to God, "Father, the weight that I feel is in no comparison to any weight that is found in a gym." The weight of the world has a different magnitude attached to it. The weight of your circumstance becomes unbearable when you no longer have any control over it. You cannot hold it.

The LORD reminded me of Jesus' crucifixion. He suffered the ultimate sacrifice. His sacrifice was a service to God. He served in excruciating pain while being silent. When the sins of the world were released on his shoulders, He cried, "My God! My God! Why have you forsaken me?" When sin was released on Jesus, the Bible says that God departed from Him; and that's when He cried out to God. The pain and weight from His service and sacrifice became unbearable when God departed from Him.

I began to realize that I, too, was handling things without God. It was a hard pill to swallow, but truth is I chose when to let God in. Additionally, I expected God to work a miracle when all of the faculties of my body were not submitted to Him. My heart wanted to come to Him and was aware of His presence; however, my mind hindered total submission to Him. I was carrying what He desired for me to give to Him.

God works miracles when every faculty of our being is totally submitted to Him. The Bible tells us that Jesus did not do more miracles while He was here on earth due to the unbelief in the hearts of people. God desires to work on your behalf, but you must be completely surrendered. Your mind, heart, and spirit must be in accord with Him.

Once you completely submit to God, then it will become easier to serve with excellence. It won't matter what is taking place in your surroundings because every area of your life will revolve around Him. Therefore, your surroundings must respond to Him. He will take the weight away and give you grace to do what is purposed in your heart—with excellence. Will you feel the pain while serving? Absolutely! However, the weight of what you would normally carry will be lifted and you will have access God's divine peace and joy as you serve.

You may be thinking that this is farfetched, but this is accessible to all. Choose not to compromise in your service to God by telling the pain from your situation to HUSH!

CHAPTER SEVENTEEN

SILENCE BIRTHS GRATITUDE

Gratitude: the quality for being thankful; readiness to show appreciation for and to return kindness: THANKFULNESS.

It was about 7:30am when I found myself in the stillness of God's presence. I began to worship Him for His extensive character that He shows us on a daily basis. Then I began to praise Jesus for His blood and the power that lies within it. I paused to digest it. Have you ever just sat in silence to *really* think about the power that is encompassed in the Blood of Jesus?

I continued in thanking Him and began declaring that His Blood was enough for me. For it is Jesus' Blood that saves us. His blood delivers us. His blood cleanses us.

I am reminded of the story in Luke about the paralytic man who was lowered down through the roof of a house where Jesus was ministering. To the carnal eye, this man needed healing, but Jesus saw things by the Spirit.

"When He saw their faith, He said to him, "Man, your sins are forgiven you." (Luke 5:20 NKJV)

The Bible goes on to say that, the Pharisees began to think "What in the world?" They were confused as to why Jesus did not address the obvious problem. Jesus knew what they were thinking and responded by saying:

"...'Why are you reasoning in your hearts? Which is easier, to say, 'Your sins are forgiven you' or to say, 'Rise up and walk'? But that you may know that the Son of Man has power on earth to forgive sins' —He said to the man who was paralyzed, 'I say to you arise, take up your bed, and go to your house.'" (Luke 5:22-24 NKJV)

As a result, the man who was once paralyzed responded to Jesus' voice by getting up and walking home. Jesus' vision goes much deeper than what our natural eyes can see. His primary purpose was not to feed the hearts of spectators, but instead, to address what people really needed. More than healing, this man needed forgiveness.

When we praise God, we sometimes limit our praise to things we have seen Him do in our lives when the greater miracle is in those things which we cannot see. Therefore, when I praise God for the blood of Jesus, I think about all the things that I did not see, yet Christ's blood reached beyond my sight and rescued me. His blood was the atonement for my sins—past, present, future.

As I sat in silence, an overwhelming sense of gratitude came over me. His blood protects us from all the schemes of the enemy—even the hidden ones. I was reminded of the many efforts made by the enemy to either stop or kill me. Three significant instances took place in my life where I am eternally grateful for God's protection. I will share two of those instances with you.

The First Instance

On Monday, August 4, 1986, a family was returning to their Florida home after taking a brief getaway. The family of six entered their home and decided to rest after their extensive drive. The husband and wife duo had two children at the time; an energetic and curious toddler boy, and a beautiful, quiet baby girl. As the mother was preparing to put their daughter down for a nap, there was a knock at the door. Puzzled as to who would know that they just arrived home, they were very apprehensive in answering. Upon opening the door, they found that it was their neighbor: a nineteen-year-old woman who resided in the Bahamas but would visit her friend often in Florida. This young woman came over to the couple's home frequently to feed her infatuation with the couple's infant daughter. The couple decided to let her in and as routine when she came to visit, she bypassed the couple's toddler son, and made her way to the baby girl. As the nineteen-year-old held the couple's baby girl, she knew that she had to have her.

She moved forward with planning a scheme to take the baby. The young woman stated to the couple that she needed to make a phone call at a pay phone a few yards from the couple's home and asked if she could take their baby girl with her. As any parent would respond, the couple's answer was a unanimous no. The nineteen-year-old continued to beg. At that point, the father of the infant stated that the baby was cranky from the trip and needed a nap. After much begging, the couple apprehensively agreed to allow this young woman to take their baby for a quick phone call as long as she came right back. The young woman left, and the couple waited.

After several minutes had passed, the father knew something was wrong. He left his home with his father-in-law to the place this young woman allegedly said she would be. When he arrived, his heart sank, and reality hit. The young woman and his baby girl were not there. Although he did not want to admit it, he knew in his gut that his precious baby girl had been kidnapped.

The nineteen-year-old called three of her friends who rented a Buick and asked them to take her to the Miami Airport where she purchased a ticket to Nassau, Bahamas with Eastern Airlines.

Meanwhile, the father rushed home in a panic. He and his father-in-law grabbed their weapons because they were determined to get their baby back. The father told his wife that their baby was abducted. Although she was still in denial as to what had taken place, this young wife proceeded to call the police. She also reached out to friends all over the nation and asked for prayer for the safe return of her baby. They had no idea that their baby was out of the country.

After working with the police for hours, they became frustrated as the police were only trained to do so much with kidnappings. Seeing the desperate mother's agony, a sergeant recommended that the couple get in contact with the Adam Walsh Foundation. The couple contacted the Adam Walsh foundation who continued searching and working diligently toward a safe return of the couple's baby.

The couple finally went home to try to rest. However, when they turned on the television their baby girl's picture flashed across the screen. Not knowing the magnitude of what was happening, their toddler son said,

"Hey! That's my sister!"

Pain gripped the couple's hearts once again. They could not escape their painful reality. All they had was their faith.

The nineteen-year-old and infant arrived in the Bahamas at about 6:30pm. Once she arrived at her apartment with the baby, she received a call from her friend who lived in the same neighborhood as the infant's parents. Her friend asked the nineteen-year-old if she had the couple's child, which she denied. Her friend then warned her that the police were everywhere, and if she had the child, then it would be best for her to turn herself in.

The nineteen-year-old began to have second thoughts and scheduled a flight to Miami Airport at 9:45am the next morning. Upon arriving to the airport, the nineteen-year-old turned herself in to the Miami Police. After thirty-one hours, the baby was recovered, and reunited with her parents.

Why did I share this story? Because I am that baby girl. I was abducted from my family when I was an infant, but because of God's grace and promise over my life, I was safely returned into the right hands.

So, in this moment where I was sitting with an abundance of gratitude to God, I thought about this abduction. I thought about how God protected me even then. He protected me when I did not know better. Years later, I learned that He would also protect me when I knew better.

The Second Instance

I had just celebrated my twenty-first birthday and was driving a brand-new car that my parents purchased for me. I also just graduated Bible School and accepted the call of God on my life to minister. My wedding was only four months away, so in preparation I met my father at a store called SYMS. SYMS was a place where my father purchased the majority of his suits. He planned to purchase a few suits that day; so, I told him I would join him before my sister and I headed north to check on a friend who was recovering from a freak accident. My father purchased a few suits, we said our goodbyes, and went our separate ways.

As I was driving north on the interstate, my sister and I began to talk and reminisce about the old secular songs that we used to listen to while we were growing up. I still had a few CD's, so I told her to grab one of my mixes so that we could sing to them.

I inserted the CD, and it was full of foul and derogatory language. However, because of my desire to relive days that had gone by, I turned it up! We sang and rapped our hearts out! Then, Holy Spirit arrested me. He said, "Turn it off." I stopped singing abruptly, but my sister was still singing her little heart out. So, I ignored Him and joined back in with my sister. Holy Spirit stopped me again, and said, "Turn it off." At this point, I was a little concerned. Therefore, instead of turning the music off, I turned it down. Still singing and rapping, I exited off the interstate and came to a red light. Holy Spirit spoke again and said, "Turn it off." This time I blatantly disobeyed Holy Spirit by turning it up and kept on driving.

I was about ten minutes away from my friend's home. As I was making a left turn, a storm came out of nowhere. Violent winds and heavy rains caused my car to slide under the back of a truck. The CD popped out of the CD player, and my other CD's were scattered on the floor. The driver of the pick-up truck got out of her vehicle and told my sister and I to get into her truck for safety. However, my sister did not move. She was apprehensive about getting out because the weather was so violent. I convinced her to get out, and we ran to safety (which happened to be the other driver's truck).

Once we got in, we were caught in the middle of what was later discovered to be a tornado. The truck began to rock from side to side, and we were unable to see anything. My sister was crying for fear of our lives. Being convicted of my blatant disobedience, I began to repent, and pray for our safety aloud. The driver of the car began talking about what to do next, however what was next was not on my mind. My greatest focus was making it through what was going on then. I kept on praying aloud, and the other driver eventually stopped talking.

The stormed passed over after about two or three minutes, and the sun was shining again as if nothing happened. We exited the truck and found that my brand-new car was totaled; however, the airbags did not deploy. We should have had significant injuries, but we walked away unharmed. The LORD protected my sister and I— even in my disobedience, and for that, I am forever grateful.

My time of reflection ignited gratitude in my heart for God's grace, mercy, and faithfulness towards me. I am sure that you can also think of times where God protected you from dangers seen and unseen. This type of protection speaks of the love that God has for us.

Take a moment to get quiet. Tell your thoughts to HUSH. Tell your pain to HUSH. Tell every distraction to HUSH, and just sit and think. Think of all of the times God shielded you. He shielded you when you did not know better. He shielded you when you knew better. What a Mighty God we serve!

In the space provided below, I want you to write down the times when God protected you. Think about times where He shielded you from danger. As you write, may your heart be filled with gratitude. May the joy of God fill your soul, and your voice speak of His praise!

_____

_____

_____

_____

_____

_____

_____

_____

_____

_____

_____

_____

HUSH Girl!

HUSH Girl!

IN CONCLUSION

This entire book came from a post I made on Facebook on July 7, 2020:

"I see a lot, and I would like to say a lot BUT Holy Spirit stops me with a simple, 'Hush girl.'..."

This post was really exposing my desire and temptation to give my harmless "two-cents", however Holy Spirit would not release me to do so. I am not exactly sure as to why, but I know that the purpose behind His instruction was connected to my destiny.

The same holds true with you. Your "two-cents" may be harmless in your eyes, but can I share something with you? Your current vision does not encompass your future. Your vision does not extend out as far as God's vision; additionally, your vision may not end when God's vision for you ends. There may be a lot of gray area in your vision. You may be unclear about the details of the process required to get to your destined place. This is why it is so important that you remain close to God in your questionable seasons. Only God knows the details of your life and, believe it or not, the details are connected to your communication. Let me break it down:

The details of your life are connected to your tongue (what you allow to come out of your mouth), who you are connected with (such as friends and alliances), and what you are associated with (i.e. what you share on your social media accounts). God knows how one misunderstanding can change the entire direction of your life. In the same manner, He knows that one bold statement can dramatically shift your life. With that said, sometimes He will tell you to press the brakes in order to preserve your future.

God will call you to silent moments for the sake of developing, protecting, and positioning you for greater. Do not deny the process because of your limited understanding—submit to God instead. Be obedient in the midst of pain, because in the end, you will see that it was a setup for greater.

You have the right to remain silent, even in the questionable seasons of life. Hush Girl!

THE ANSWER

The answer: Our words hold power. I *had* to be quiet in the most questionable and painful seasons of my life because I was underdeveloped, and my words could have spoken contrary to the purpose that God set before me. I experienced disappointment after disappointment. I would become hopeful only to see the door shut in my face. I was crushed over, and over, and over again.

One morning, I was watching a video of a young woman who was talking about how the LORD *had to* force her out of situations for her good. Then the LORD spoke to me:

"Daughter you are in a season of My favor. I had to shut the door because if given the opportunity to introduce yourself, the opportunity would have been yours. But those opportunities aren't in My will for you. I have something much bigger. You're only going to get there through complete abandonment of what you think you need."

I say to you, do not become discouraged when doors close without explanation. Do not become discouraged when people leave without explanation. Do not become disheartened when you are not able to explain yourself or speak on a situation. I am very familiar with the frustration, the pain, and the weight that comes with this—however, this is all a part of carrying your cross.

You have to be silent because you may risk speaking based on your pain. Your destiny cannot not thrive on words of pain. The only way that you will get through this season of silence is through complete obedience to God. He holds your future. Your future is attainable if you can endure your NOW. I have learned that sometimes the best way to get through painful seasons is by being silent.

I encourage you that when it is hard to speak, remain connected to God. It is necessary that you submit to God completely. God has something much bigger that is only developed through your silence.

Trust the silence.

HUSH Girl!

PRAYER & DECLARATIONS

I choose to put on the garment of praise for the spirit of heaviness. Heaviness has to go because the King of Glory is here with me. Father, You reign on the throne of my life and I praise Your Holy Name. You are Mighty! You are Good! There is no one who can compare to You! My soul boasts in You. Your praise will be on my lips!

I will bless the LORD, O my soul and everything that is within me! Thank You for Your love. Thank You for Your joy. Thank You for Your peace! Father, You are Great and greatly to be praised! Be exalted in my life.

I decree and declare that the LORD, my God is in my midst. He is the Mighty One Who will save, and He is rejoicing over me with gladness. He is quieting me by His love. I command my pain to be quiet. I command my anxieties to be quiet. I command all distractions to be quiet and I decree that I will rest in God's love. (Action: Inhale slowly. Exhale slowly). I decree and declare that I am resting in Your love Father. Exalt over me with loud singing and silence my enemies.

Let God arise and His enemies be scattered! I am safe in Your love Father. Thank You for Your protection and safety.

I decree and declare that I will not be anxious about tomorrow. I will not be anxious about what I cannot control or see. I command my soul to rest in the Peace of God. May Jehovah Shalom (The LORD my Peace) stand at the gateway of my heart, mind and soul. Peace is my portion. Father I declare Your Word that says:

"Peace I leave with you; My peace I give to you. Not as the world gives do I give to you. Let not your hearts be troubled, neither let them be afraid." (John 14:27)

I receive Your peace and declare that I will not walk in fear. I will walk in the confidence of Your Word and Your promises. In Jesus' Name.

I cast my burden on You LORD. You will sustain me. I find my strength in You to stand even in life's most difficult seasons. You will never permit that I am moved. Therefore, I stand. I do not lose heart. I trust You for You are my Sustainer.

You are my Refuge. You are my Stronghold and Present Help in the time of trouble. I draw closer to You. You are my Anchor and You are Faithful to keep me stable. My eyes are focused on You.

Your Word says that those who seek You will lack no good thing. So, Father I praise You for greater. I praise You for doors opening. I praise You for the Heavens opening. I praise You for the blessings that will manifest after I endure for a little while. Thank You for opening up pathways and opportunities that no man can shut down. You are Faithful to Your Word; therefore, I rejoice in You, and You alone.

You are my Everlasting Rock Father. I will seek You for You are my Hiding Place. You are my Strength. You will protect me from trouble and surround me with Your songs of deliverance.

Father deliver me from the bondage of the enemy. For Your Word declares that He Who the Son sets free is free indeed. I decree and declare that I am free from fear. I decree and declare that I am free from insecurity. I decree and declare that I am free from anger and frustration. I decree and declare that I am free from pride. I decree and declare that I am free from all addictions. I decree and declare that I am free from infirmity. By Your stripes, I am healed! I decree and declare that I am free from the opinions of others. I decree and declare that every word curse, and every negative diagnosis is broken off my life!

I decree and declare that I will walk in an abundance of love, grace, joy and peace. I decree and declare that I shall reap a harvest and see the Your goodness in the land of the living.

I speak life to myself. I speak life to my seed. I speak life to my surroundings and immediate environment.

Father send Your glory so that people will know that You are still the Living and True God. Father, I thank You for going before me. Thank You for fighting for me. Thank You for being with me.

My hope and confidence are in You. You never fail. I love You LORD. I declare that because You are on my side, that I SHALL NOT be defeated! In Jesus' Name. Amen!

Scripture References:

Zephaniah 3:17; Matthew 6:34; John 14:27; Psalm 55:22; Psalm 9:9-10; Psalm 34:10; Isaiah 26:3-4; 1 Chronicles 16:11; Psalm 32:7-8; Deuteronomy 31:8

HUSH Girl!

What Did You Think of "HUSH Girl!"?

Thank you for purchasing **"HUSH Girl!"**. You could have picked any number of books to read, but you chose this book; and for that I am extremely grateful.

It is my prayer that **"HUSH Girl!"** has added value and quality to your daily life. If so, then it would be really nice if you could do *at least* one of the following:

1. Post a review on Amazon.com
2. Share this book with your friends and family
3. Share this book on Facebook, Instagram, and/or Twitter and hashtag #HUSHgirl

If you have enjoyed **"HUSH Girl!"** and found benefit in reading it, I'd love to hear from you and hope that you could take some time to post a review, and share it with others.

My prayers are with you and your loved ones. May you be enriched with God's blessings forevermore.

For information on booking Tiffany, please visit www.simplytiffany.net.

CPSIA information can be obtained
at www.ICGtesting.com
Printed in the USA
JSHW031216310121
11379JS00001B/4

9 781735 922201